GENESIS AMARIS KEMP

CHOCOLATE DROP IN CORPORATE AMERICA

FROM THE PIT TO THE PALACE

Genesis Amaris Kemp

CHOCOLATE DROP IN CORPORATE AMERICA

FROM THE PIT TO THE PALACE

Genesis Amaris Kemp

Pearly Gates Publishing LLC
INSPIRING CHRISTIAN AUTHORS TO BE AUTHORS

Pearly Gates Publishing, LLC, Houston, Texas

Chocolate Drop in Corporate America

Chocolate Drop in Corporate America
From the Pit to the Palace

Copyright © 2020
Genesis Amaris Kemp

ISBN 13: 978-1-948853-20-0
2nd Edition, January 27, 2021 | 1st Edition Published May 26, 2020
Library of Congress Control Number: 2021901670

Some identifying details have been changed to
protect the privacy of individuals.

For information and bulk ordering, contact:
Pearly Gates Publishing, LLC
Angela Edwards, CEO
P.O. Box 62287
Houston, TX 77205
BestSeller@PearlyGatesPublishing.com

Dedication

**To Venessa, my Spiritual Angel,
my ride-or-die, my bestie, my little sister:**
Even though you aren't physically here, I know
you are smiling down from Heaven. Your legacy
and impact will **ALWAYS** live on.
This is for you and future generations to come.

Chocolate Drop in Corporate America is also
dedicated to every admin who was told they
would never get out of the box — the one that the
corporation places around you because they
don't recognize your value and can't see past
general administrative tasks. Admins, you are
more than "just an admin." Use your current
situation to catapult you to your rightful
platform.

To every minority who has struggled to
find their rightful place in Corporate America, I
dedicate this book to you as well. You are the ones
who had to constantly fight for a seat at the table,
work twice as hard even to be seen and noticed,
and feel invaluable as if you are just a number to
the corporation. Eventually, you find that one

divine connection who can see your worth. Only then do you get a breakthrough.

To every business professional in all walks of life, you are not forgotten. Everyone has faced and endured various trials and tribulations that could be spoken about, some of which were unfair, while others you turned from a negative into a positive. You have been emboldened to launch out deep and walk into your destiny, purpose, and calling.

To those who are willing to take off the blinders, do some self-reflection, and work on creating lasting change in the workforce: Know that if we do not speak up, stand, call out unconscious biases, and work on changing the mindset of those ignorant individuals, then we are only regressing instead of moving forward in society. Let's all come together and work collaboratively to make lasting impacts.

Lastly, I dedicate this book to everyone who has a dream not to let people or things keep you in bondage. Follow your heart, share your story, travel, and be the best version of yourself. Someone needs you to pass the baton, be their voice, narrate their story, or partner with them to create a revolution of opportunities.

Acknowledgments

First and foremost, I thank God for planting inside me the seed to write and the ability to use my words and experiences to bring hope to those in need.

I would like to honor my parents for instilling in me good Christian values and telling me to continually pray and trust God in all situations, despite how it looks in the natural. Having both my parents in my life has been truly inspirational. I don't know where I'd be today without them.

To my Boaz/My Rock/My Boo/My Husband: I thank you for always being by my side to lend an ear to hear, compliment me, challenge me to see things from various perspectives, and to be real and honest when needed (even though it may hurt).

I thank my brothers and their wives for always challenging me, believing in me, giving me words of encouragement, and showing me tough love when needed.

I thank my friends who encouraged me to keep writing and to share my story because there may be someone else going through similar situations that needs this message. Prayerfully, this book will give them the ability to keep pushing forward, strengthen themselves, and provide a heightened awareness to look for other opportunities.

For all who discounted and discredited me, I thank you for pushing me into my new season to write and share my testimony with others. If you weren't a thorn in my side, I wouldn't have been pricked to write and express myself.

I thank everyone mentioned here — no matter their role in my life — because they have all been pivotal key players in my development and shaping me to be the woman I am today.

Preface

Genesis started writing out of frustration. Little did she know that what began as a short blurb would catapult her to writing a full-blown book. Writing down her frustrations, discontent, anger, and unhappiness was her way to grieve and cope with her current work situation. It was also God wanting her to birth and release content that would shake the atmosphere, allow others to see a different perspective from theirs, educate others on what really takes place in Corporate America with minorities, and let people know they are not alone in their trials and tribulations.

We all face various situations in the workplace that may not be "politically correct," fair, or whatever the case may be, but it does not mean you need to shrink back and tolerate the mistreatment. Speak up and work on creating change because it's not always about us, but rather those coming behind, beside, and future generations to come.

Introduction

While reading Chocolate Drop in Corporate America, Genesis is going to take you through her journey of working at a Fortune 500 company — a big name company that talks a good game about "Valuing their personnel," "Inclusion," and "Diversity." Meanwhile, you are on the inside, enduring relentless trials and tribulations. That's not unique, though. As a matter of fact, it's much like any other company. Here's the thing: Times have changed. Certain things are no longer acceptable or tolerated because there are now various outlets and organizations available to defend and speak on your behalf if needed.

It's not a catwalk like "they" make it seem. One you are reeled in, they try to condition you to make their way the only plausible one.

Think about either your current or past career situations when you felt as if you faced numerous difficulties and didn't really have an outlet on which to rely. You couldn't go to Human Resources because they, of course, are looking out for the best interest of the company.

Management is nonchalant and hands-off, and nothing is truly "anonymous." As a result, you remained quiet and endured the mistreatment because the pay was decent, and you had great benefits. Pretty much, you sacrificed your morals and values at the expense of your true happiness.

How did it affect your mental, physical, and emotional state? Why didn't you have the courage to speak up or work towards changing your situation to ensure you get peace of mind, are paid what you are worth, and be made to feel valuable—versus being just another number or box for them to check off that demonstrates they employ specific demographics criteria?

This book was written to encourage you to be bold and courageous. Fight for what's right! Never settle because there is someone out there who needs you to be a change agent to pave the way for them. Where you start does not have to be where you end up. If you are willing to put in the work, the sky is the limit! However, failure to recognize "they" will never truly value you will be a failure to walk into your destiny.

Sometimes, it's during those difficult times when there is a lesson in the midst of redirecting us — an experience that will yield a better outcome for our lives. Choose today not to remain complacent. Step outside of your comfort zone and give a voice to whatever ails you! Speak up for what's right! Be fearless in your pursuit to share your testimony with others! One step at a time, build your empire and legacy. This world needs **YOU**!

God does not make mistakes, and He will never leave or forsake us.

Table of Contents

Chapter 1

The Pit...The Beginning...2013

Woohoo! **YAY!** This Chocolate Drop was on the move! It was my first day in the Ivy League or (as some would say) the Big Boys & Girls Club! I was finally #*ADULTING*. My level of joy was immeasurable as I began working for a Fortune 500 company — a big-time, billion-dollar entity known worldwide. My new position brought with it all the accolades that were attached to the company's easily recognizable name. Alas, my work background, experience, and skills were paying off!

I already had my Associate's Degree and was pursuing my Bachelor's. However, it wasn't until all the hype died down and reality set in that I realized my previous Oil and Gas experience landed me the job interview, which led to a job offer. There was one problem, though: They wanted me to do less than that which I was qualified, although my background included technical expertise and some HSE (Health, Safety, and Environmental).

Mind you: I was **HOT** on the employment block. I had *THREE* job offers on the table, and this company was the lowest-paying of the bunch.

I contemplated for a while on which position to accept because, in the natural, those high-paying positions sounded really good — especially in terms of career advancement and an increased salary. My flesh wanted to chase the money because I was young at the time and wanted to be able to afford certain things on my own. All I saw was $$$s and what I could do with all that green to advance my goals and, of course, build the Kingdom of God.

I needed spiritual confirmation that I was heading in the right direction. So, before I even made my decision, I did what any mature Christian would do: I sought out wise counsel from my parents and pastor. I wanted to talk to someone who has been through the situation before.

NOTE: It's always good to get wise counsel and use wisdom when you are stepping into unfamiliar territory.

Fast-forward...

I ended up choosing this particular company based on their longevity, brand, status quo, and with the hopes of moving up, despite the entry-level position and low salary. I thought it was the best way to get my foot in the door.

Enter yet another problem: When I started to inquire about career paths and personal development, I felt stuck. Even though I was hired as an Administrative Assistant (AA), I believed I should've still had a career path to follow to advance and grow within the company. After all, who in their right mind would want to be stuck in the same position if they don't have to be?

Now, if you love what you do and want to continue doing it, that's great! However, if you are ambitious, don't settle for less. Gain understanding and clarity. Be willing to challenge the system and its limitations.

As for me, I was an ambitious one. I sought out mentors, worked my ass off, did step-out activities, took training courses, and the list goes on. Pretty much, I checked off each item on their big "To-Do List" they provide but don't necessarily advise on what it really takes to help accelerate through the ranks. When I asked some seasoned admins and other up-and-comers for advice (since I was still seen as "The New Girl" or "Fresh Air Kid"), I kept hearing the same damn lines:

> ➢ *"Once an Admin, ALWAYS an Admin."*
> ➢ *"It's very hard to get out of the box."*

BOX? What 'BOX'?

They then went on to explain the various all-encompassing roles of the "OCA" and "MPT."

OCA is Office, Clerical, and Administrative roles—the paraprofessionals, admins, technicians…and whatever else the company deems fit.

MPT is Managerial, Professional, and Technical roles—the Engineers, Chemists, Geoscientists, Geologists, Supervisors, Managers, etc.

The MPTs have a career path that is obviously inconsistent with the rest of the company. I wonder, *"Why is that?"* Think about it! Why does one group have career-planning, and the other does not? It's as if they don't even care about the admins or technicians. **SHOCKING!!!** That is definitely not what I expected from a company of such high caliber and accolades!

After digesting what I heard, I realized the news did not sit well with me or my spirit-woman. It was **WRONG** and needed to be addressed—and fixed *expeditiously*! I knew there was more inside of me and was not about to settle for anything less than God's best for my life. Daily, I reminded myself that I was going to move up and defy the odds. I knew in my heart that I was **NOT** going to remain an admin for long. I was determined and knew I was going to prove them **ALL** wrong, as well as overcome any stigmas they had of me.

I was just getting started. It was just the beginning!

Chapter 2

Getting Down to Business

Cracking the Whip

While on my daily grind doing routine administrative tasks, I began to look up all the company perks. I wanted to know what incentives they had to offer their employees. Mind you: I was still getting my base work done in the interim, but I also needed to learn the ins and outs about the corporation, too. When you work for a Fortune 500 company with a big brand, you are branded by association and receive certain perks from partner companies, such as specific employee discounts. Without researching and knowing the benefits and perks the company has to offer, you may be left in the dark.

It just goes to show that not everything will be given to you on a silver platter with a golden spoon. Some things you must seek out for yourself. As they say, **KNOWLEDGE is POWER!**

With me being a Chocolate Drop in a sea of Creamy White Chocolate, Marshmallows, and Caramel Macchiatos, I had to step it up. I had to increase my knowledge, learn various policies, and fire on all cylinders. I was being put to the test because they wanted to see just how long I would last. I had to bring my A-game because I stood out like that bright yellow bird on Sesame Street. Four additional factors played against me:

1. I am Chocolate.
2. I am a woman.
3. I was the youngest on my team.
4. All the colleagues on my team were older vanilla males (at the time).

When I began to prove myself, earn my rank, demand respect, and lay down some basic ground rules, things started to run smoothly. I had to make it known I wasn't like the other admins they had in the past and that as I learn and make improvements to the processes, things may or may not be the same. I was hired to be an Administrative Assistant, not a *PERSONAL* Assistant. (There were personal tasks I refused to do for others, as they were not in my job description.)

Once I found my groove, they knew my limits, and I understood their work preferences and personalities, I felt like some of the barriers came down. I was able to open up to some of the male colleagues (and vice-versa), we were able to bond, and it genuinely felt like a family.

My boss, on the other hand, was a bit rigid at times, hard to read, and seemed far removed from the team. He stayed in his own lane — *BOXED* in. It was a lot like pulling teeth to get information out of him. There was a time when I requested one-on-one sessions so that we can check in with each other, either on a weekly or monthly basis, to discuss my projects, changes with the team, request performance feedback, and so forth. Our meetings were somewhat inconsistent. He was very nonchalant and often seemed mentally and emotionally removed from the team and the job as a whole.

There was one time in particular when something rose in me like a lion ready to hunt prey. I went into my boss' office and explained that I would like to explore potential growth opportunities. I told him I was in school and that my goals and aspirations did not include being a "paper-pusher" or Administrative Assistant for the long term. During that conversation, he began to display signs that he cared or was at least willing to help me. We discussed what I was currently majoring in, and when I told him, *"Psychology,"* he replied, *"What do you plan on doing with Psychology working here? You aren't going to go far with that degree."* Although I was a bit discouraged, I continued to listen. After all, feedback is a gift that you can use to digest what is applicable while discarding the rest.

So, he went on to tell me that the company has tuition reimbursement, but to receive approval, it is solely for degrees that can be applied to one's current position or to advance one's career within the company. He advised me to speak with my advisor to see what degrees were offered at the college campus. I was already taking night classes, so I could work full-time while pursuing my degree via a satellite campus.

So, there I was…a non-traditional student who was juggling work and school. It was not easy, but it needed to be done. I had no time to waste because I had goals and dreams to fulfill, and time waits for **NO ONE.** I was grateful for the advice and feedback because he did not have to share any of it with me.

Remember: Feedback is a *gift*. You can either accept or discard it. However, be glad someone cared enough to share with you. It's up to you to discern whether or not it applies to your situation or is in your best interest.

Chapter 3

The Leap of Faith

I walked into the University of Houston's Advising Office and asked to speak to an Advisor. I gave them the rundown and then asked what degrees were offered at their location, as well as inquiring about whether they cater to full-time employees who need to take night classes. They presented me with two degree options: "Mechanical Engineering in Technology" and "Supply Chain and Logistics Technology." I then asked, *Out of the two degrees, which one will accept some or most of the core classes I already completed under my Psychology degree plan?* I was not about to waste money and not have some of my courses transfer over since I would technically be moving from the College of Liberal Arts and Social Studies (CLASS) to the College of Technology (COT).

I needed to understand and get clarification before returning to work the next day. I wanted to have all the facts and my ducks in a row when I approached my boss. He was the type of man who needed **FACTS** and was not keen on people wasting his time. Needless to say, all my facts were in order, and I was ready for round two of our discussion.

When I went to work the next day, I told my boss I was ready to continue our discussion. I handed him the two degree plans, and he glanced at them briefly. It took some time before he even acknowledged them (I suppose he was in his analysis phase). He then gave me his opinion on what roles within the company would be tied to Mechanical Engineering Technology. Since it was not an Engineering Degree per se, the company may not recognize me as an Engineer if I chose that degree, but it would open some doors. Regarding Supply Chain and Logistics Technology, he described what roles I could potentially move into within the company, including Procurement, Supply Chain, or Logistics (to name a few). He also stated the company would pay tuition reimbursement for either degree; I just had to choose which one would be most beneficial for me.

I made my choice, put in a request to change my major, and submitted my pre-enrollment forms to my boss for him to approve. Once he granted his approval, it was then sent to the Benefits Administration Department. Everything needed to be approved by them before enrolling in courses or tuition would not be reimbursed.

Finally, I was on my way! My goal of getting out of the admin world and into the professional — once I completed my degree — was becoming a reality! *Talk about a leap of faith!* I changed my entire degree plan and shifted gears to appease the company's standards with the hopes of advancing my career. They were investing in me, so you would think they would want to yield a return on their investment, correct?

Chapter 4

Three Years in the Making

The Father, The Son, and The Holy Spirit

I changed my degree from Psychology to Supply Chain and Logistics Technology. I went from the College of Liberal Arts and Social Studies to the College of Technology — from left to right, easy to hard...Beauty to Beast.

I knew it was going to take hard work, determination, and perseverance to complete the degree. For three years, I had to continue juggling work and school. I worked diligently while participating in extracurricular activities to strengthen my performance review and ranking, networking with others, and building credibility.

During that time, a lot of other changes occurred. My first male supervisor moved on to another role. I got a new female boss, which meant we had to learn each other's work ethics, preferences, and styles. I shared with her my goals and aspirations and learned how she wanted and needed me to assist her as an Administrative Assistant. She raised the bar and required a little more out of me than my previous boss, which was fine because I didn't mind being stretched and learning new things. The team dynamics changed, too, as new people rotated in and out of the group, requiring me to support the newcomers as well.

In addition to all of that, I had to change my work schedule a bit to fit my class schedule. Everything was fine and dandy. I was meeting metrics, received excellent performance reviews and peer feedbacks, got my little raises, and took necessary training courses. Then, more changes came down the pipe, including an increase in responsibilities. I started supporting two managers and two groups. Disappointingly, there was not an increase in my salary because the change was part of the company restructuring. (If they hired another admin to help carry the load, they would have paid him or her a set salary, so I'm unsure why they chose not to bump up my salary. Talk about doing more with less!)

As one who is always mindful of my progress (or lack thereof), I interpreted the "change" as a sign meant for me to pay closer attention to the way the company was treating me. Thankfully, my second and third managers were wonderful. The new male boss came from a different background and was part of a different organization before the restructure. It was great to learn some new methods and be challenged by him. He pushed me not to settle and spoke into my life with encouraging words and more.

It's funny how God will allow different people to come into your life at divine times and for certain seasons. Some people come to teach, some to challenge, some to grow you, some to be a connector, some to listen, some for you to minister to, and others to help fund your visions or goals.

Within those three years, I experienced a host of changes. My personal growth was on the rise, and I was near the end of my degree pursuit.

Chapter 5

The Walk and Hats Off

A little glimmer of hope was shining through, the sun was bursting through the dark skies, and God was emerging, letting me know He was there with me every step of the way, especially when I thought He was far versus near. During those years, it sometimes felt as if the walls were closing in, and my feet were running fast to escape the trap. That was when God swooped in to let me know He still had me in the palms of His hands.

Those three years really flew by. As 2016 was winding down, year-end work was ramping up. I had to ensure all fourth quarter duties were closed out timely. I can't forget to mention that graduation was around the corner. It seemed as if everything was moving quickly, much like a horse on a racetrack. I was filled with mixed emotions. Nervousness, excitement, fear, and anxiety rose to the top. The combination of those feelings felt like I was on an endless emotional rollercoaster!

When I asked for a personal day or excused absence because my graduation day fell during the workweek, my *female* supervisor told me I would have to take a vacation day. My *male* supervisor told me it could be excused (at the time, the female supervisor was my primary manager and lead, so her ruling took precedence; however, before the restructure, the male supervisor had a higher rank). In response to the confusion, I looked up the company policy and found some guidelines applied to my situation. That revelation caused me to pause. If something was clearly written in black and white, why were the rules different for Chocolate Drops versus Vanilla Drops? The guidelines should be the same across the board, no matter what, correct? In no way should the decision be based on the discretion of the manager when the rules concerning leave are written for all to see.

For instance, if a manager allows an individual to take a personal (or excused) day to take their animal to the vet, then why wouldn't the same be true for a valid reason — such as my graduation day?! During my tenure, I have observed people getting excused time off for some of the most bogus reasons.

So, with me being a fighter for justice, I challenged the manager's decision, especially since the company was paying for my tuition.

They invested in me, so it didn't make sense for them not to let me have an "off the record" day.

The lesson I learned here was that it just goes to show there are rules that apply for some but not necessarily for others.

In Corporate America, there are times when things aren't consistent. In this day and age, there is a lot of favoritism, nepotism, ageism, sexism, racial injustice, unconscious bias, and even segregation to a degree. If you don't speak up for yourself, don't expect others to do it for you. In some cases, you may have an advocate or sponsor who absolutely sees your potential and genuinely wants to see you succeed. If not, you must be that voice, but make sure you do it tactfully so as not to ruffle any feathers or become pigeon-holed.

Sadly, double-standards always apply as it relates to Chocolate Drops — whether Creamy, Dark, or Crunchy. Speaking in general, it's like that with minorities across the board. If you speak up loudly or too frequently, you will get labeled as "AGGRESSIVE," which we all know is a load of crap. That's especially true if one of our counterparts places us in a "BOX" and says, *"Oh, that's just how 'they' are."* It all comes down to the trivial versus the extreme. I say, ***"If it's a cat, then call it a cat!"*** Don't make excuses for one and not the other.

In the end, I got what I wanted — in a sense. I was able to work from home versus going into the office. I then left to attend my graduation. I graduated Magna Cum Laude with a B.S. in Supply Chain and Logistics Technology, with double minors in Purchasing and Organizational Leadership & Supervision. It felt fantastic! I just knew all my hard work would pay off!

Chapter 6

Time to Move on Up

I had my degree in hand and was ready to make a move. I just knew that once I obtained my degree, I would be able to move into another role that complemented my degree. At a minimum, I felt it was my right to expect a higher salary since that's how I've seen it happen for others in the past.

Boy, was I wrong... It turned out to be yet another thing I had to fight and push for.

Once our internal system was updated to reflect my degree, I approached management to make them aware. Their response? *"We will look into it."* Well, I did not hear anything back from them for some time, even though I followed up with them time and again. It was only after I pressed hard that I received some real answers... **FINALLY!**

I came to learn the company recognizes the degree if the individual is hired on with the degree in hand already. Conversely, if you go back to pursue a degree while working at the company, it's merely for your benefit. In a nutshell, it does not mean they will recognize it and move you into a new role immediately.

One manager took some time to break down the process of what really happens once you get your degree. I was told, *"Here is the caveat: Upon obtaining a degree, it is based on the business' needs, personal interest, and some other deciding factors to get moved into a new position or recategorized into the professional bucket, which is going from OCA to MPT and, of course, your salary is tied to your classification level."* I am forever grateful to have the process explained, but something deep inside of me still felt unsettled.

I knew a few people who were in the same OCA (administrative or technician) bucket like me. They were either still in school or returned to school to obtain their degrees. Once they had their degree, the company moved them into MPT (professional roles). It's a shame how companies do things for some and not for others. Constantly advocating for yourself and challenging the system gets tiresome. The system is not always as fair as they make it seem, just as life is not always fair. In fact, a lot of Chocolate Drops and minorities end up in the same predicament — especially at the company where I work. The ones who actually get out of their respective buckets and have their classification levels raised have either an advocate or sponsor, which raises another question: How do you find an advocate or sponsor? While it is a fair question and one that many are curious about, some questions never receive a response because the company obviously doesn't believe there is an issue.

On the other hand, some are either the son or daughter of someone high in the company, have dual careers, their spouse has the leading career, they are alumni buddies, or sleep their way to the top. The saying, *It's not always about what you know, but who you know,"* is true!

What I noticed about the general Chocolate Drop population is that when they make it to a certain level, most don't even lend a hand to help those who are trying to climb the corporate ladder. Nor do they have the decency to thank those who helped them along the way. Some do, but they are an anomaly. My thought process is that if someone helped pave the way for me, then it is only right to pay it forward, especially if you know and see that young man or woman is extremely dedicated, a hard worker, possesses great work ethics, and has potential. However, not everyone thinks that way or has the same philosophy. I mean, what do you lose trying to help someone better themselves? It's just sad how things work in Corporate America. Eventually, you get to a point where you no longer want to play the game. It's all politics and a dog-eat-dog world, both of which can be emotionally and mentally draining.

For now, this is our livelihood. You and I aren't just here for fun or as a hobby. We desire to make a decent living and live comfortably, just like 'they' are. Is it wrong to want to travel like 'they' do, work on specific projects where you know you are capable of success, be credited for being an experienced hire, be adequately compensated for your experience, or whatever your personal situation may be? I, for one, do not think its wrong to know your worth and be acknowledged for it.

For example, an experienced hire (in my opinion) is anyone who has previous experience in the industry and can bring that to the table to pair it with the current work settings. Not everyone is treated like that, though, which is wrong. Therein lies a problem that needs to be addressed.

We all should be able to shoot for the stars and want to live and have that American dream. We are all valid players and components of the company. It takes all roles for the corporation to run smoothly and successfully. Once the organization realizes that, I believe it will lower the attrition rates. Employees want to feel valued and appreciated, be paid fairly, and know they are making a difference. What a difference it would make when people know they truly matter and are not just a mere number or part of a demographical box to be checked off that shows the company is managing inclusion and diversity! Without a solid foundation, the corporation would not be where it is today. The people truly make the difference.

Chapter 7

Hold Them Accountable

A few months had passed since I obtained my degree. I was still waiting to hear something back on whether they have another role where I could utilize my degree.

Why does it always feel like a waiting game? I guess the Lord is trying to instill patience in me and teach me that His will and thoughts for my life are far better than mine...which is true. It has been proven to me time and again.

I wanted to do something where I could see a return on my investment. You know...enjoy the fruits of my labor! After all, I took the time to advance my education and made sacrifices, yet it was not being put to good use by me remaining in an administrative role. Keep in mind that I already had some goals and plans in mind since I was not about to stay complacent. Nor did I want to keep waiting for something that may or may not happen. *"Time is money,"* right?

At the time, the company was already in the first quarter of 2017, and I obtained my degree in December 2016. Not only did I get a degree that aligned with some areas in the company, but I also came under their employ with a previous work history that gave me the advantage to know about certain projects this company was already working on. With that being said, I set up another meeting with management to see where we stood on the process.

It was during that meeting when I was informed two potential roles would complement my degree. Both roles were considered MPT positions and in a plant setting. I never worked in a plant setting before, so I was a little nervous. At the same time, I was glad to hear there was potential for growth. One location would require me to relocate physically, and the other would require me to make a lengthier commute than I was already making. All the while, management was still trying to work some things out in the background to ensure they had a backfill for my position, as well as placement for whatever job I did not choose. It was like a domino effect: Before moving on to the next assignment, there must be someone at the ready to tee up and take over the responsibilities — unless the position was becoming obsolete. Base work still needs to get done, and targets still need to be met.

After numerous conversations, the position that would have required me to relocate fell through, which was a blessing in disguise because I would have had to move to another state, away from my support system and family. I wasn't even sure the company would have paid relocation assistance, based on various factors. At the time, my fiancé was a factor as well, which made relocating an even more complex career situation. He was just beginning to advance in his career, so I had to be mindful of that factor. Our relationship was progressing, which meant if I relocated, I needed to be sure he would have had the ability to secure work, too. In the long run, the position that required me to commute daily to another city was the better fit at the time for my family and me. I wasn't happy about the long commute, but I wanted to advance in my career, so I sucked it up.

Sometimes in life, we are faced with making certain sacrifices to advance and get closer to reaching our goals.

Chapter 8

The Bigger the Title, The Bigger the Beast

I **did it!** I was in a position where I could utilize my Supply Chain degree and mirror it with the company's standards. That accomplishment felt fabulous because it's what I wanted. I wanted the ability to allow my degree to work for itself. I wanted to be challenged. I wanted to showcase what I learned. Most importantly, I wanted to be treated and paid like the professional I am.

Upon moving into the new role, I was told I would be on a six-month probationary period since I was crossing over from one bucket to another — from the administrative and technician pool to the professional one, which also meant there would be an increase in my salary. When I was told that, I was excited because I had hoped the company would have honored what was said. However, as I began to settle into the role and do some due diligence, other things were revealed to me (I believe it was the Holy Spirit giving me discernment). I tried to tune out the negative thoughts that floated around in my head. It was imperative that I not jeopardize my opportunity. When I heard others did not have to endure a probationary period, I was shocked! I didn't say anything, though. I just kept it cool until my probationary period was near completion. It was difficult ignoring the red flags flapping in my face, though, knowing that others did not have to endure that contingency. Why was I different? It wasn't right, and it sure wasn't fair, but as mentioned before…life isn't always fair. That stipulation was something else I filed away in the recesses of my mind as I kept making mental notes on how the company treated me.

When the six months neared the end, I told myself I was going to put them to the test to see if they would do right by me and officially convert me from OCA to MPT. Well, they didn't. When I asked why, they gave me their reasoning — some of which I agree with, and others I did not. My trainer was retiring from the company, so I had minimal training. Still, I made process improvements and ensured all materials arrived at the plant on time with no unit shutdowns or stockouts. I was already doing the work of a professional — not duties a typical admin would handle. I did, however, get nominated for some step out responsibilities. For example, I engaged with audits as a team lead and a representative for our charitable organization.

So, if I was capable of doing the work and getting it done, why was I not being treated fairly? I felt like I was being used and abused! They knew I was capable, but they insisted on keeping me in that **"BOX."** There was one particular supervisor who didn't make it any better. She had already formed a perception of me without fully giving me a chance. My gut feeling led me to believe she was "U.P." (undercover prejudice) by the way she interacted with all the Chocolate Drops. I tried to give her the benefit of the doubt, but the way she treated my predecessor was distasteful and should have been reported to Human Resources. She tried to snap at me a few times, but I politely put her in her place and nipped that in the bud. I could tell she didn't like that because she was not used to other Chocolate Drops or minorities standing against her.

At the end of the day, you still need to **RESPECT** people. There is no excuse for treating people any kind of way. It's highly unacceptable in the workplace, and certain negative behaviors should not be tolerated by anyone.

You know the disrespect is bad, especially when your colleague sitting in the next office has to come over and see if everything is okay, just because the supervisor is screaming and carrying on. It was as if her motto was, *"My way or the highway!"* If you had an idea that she didn't like or agree with, then oh well! She would say she has your best interest in mind, but her actions dictated otherwise. I couldn't trust her. It was almost like she had two personalities. One minute, she was fine; the next, she could be a terror on wheels.

That went on for a few months until she finally went on leave, and they replaced her role with a male supervisor — my fifth supervisor since being with the company. Each time I got a new manager, it was like starting over. I had to brief each on my career aspirations, background, etc., because eight times out of ten, the prior supervisor did not provide all the details. Their concerns before leaving focused on cross-training their replacement and moving into their new role. Thankfully, the new supervisor was much better to deal with. I consistently made mental notes of all interactions because he was going to be the one representing me in the performance review with other management personnel. Keep in mind that he was not there for a while, so the previous supervisor shared her input regarding me with him and the higher-ups.

When my performance review came, I was sure to address all my concerns, especially the ones concerning the previous supervisor. I was sure the input prior to her departure was not fully representative of all my accolades and considerations. During my review, I noticed another red flag. They told me I was doing a good job, that my work ethics and performance spoke for themselves, and my peers also gave me great feedback…but they just had to find a few negatives to slide in there. As a result, I wasn't converted—and it was well over the six-month probationary period. For whatever the reason, my previous supervisor had it out for me. Her perceptions were passed on to the new supervisor, and while he initially bought into some of it, it wasn't until he learned more about me and my work ethics for himself that he determined the information she provided to him was inconsistent. Due to his help, my performance review remained the same, whereas the other supervisor tried to lower it. I was ranked as a 'B' in the OCA pool, but it would have dropped to a 'C' if he did not fact check and gather his own information.

Frustration and disgust started to build inside of me. The constant change in supervisors, coupled with having to restart the career development and aspirations wheel was daunting.

At the 11 months mark, I had to have a "Come to Jesus" talk with management and ask for another assignment that was closer to home because I was spending more money on gas, tolls, and wear-and-tear on my car than I was actually making. I was paying $14 a day on tolls, countless hours in the car commuting, and was mentally drained by the time I got home — time I was never going to get back. There had to be better ways to utilize my time.

Not long before I left for vacation, management called me in and told me they found a new opportunity for me. It was a newly-created role that they said would be an excellent fit, but I would have to interview for the position. Hmm…

Another monkey wrench. Another hoop to jump through. Another red flag.

Despite what the company thought of me, I knew God had my back. I went to the interview, nailed it, and got the job!

No matter what people try to do to you, no one in Hell can stop what God has blessed and anointed!

Chapter 9

New Opportunities and Constant Grinding

The year was 2018. The number '8' is supposed to mark New Beginnings (at least in Biblical Numerology). I was stretching and exercising my faith more than ever because I just knew things would be different this time around.

I was in a newly-created role—the first of its kind for the project I would be working on. I could make the project my "baby" and really own it since I didn't have past experiences of others to live up to or overcome. I was walking blindly into unfamiliar territory, but I was ready to face the challenge head-on. I knew I was fully capable of accomplishing anything I put my mind to.

I quickly brought myself up to speed with both the internal and external stakeholders. I truly wanted to know who my key players were going to be, learn the various business lines I would interface with, and, most importantly, give people a chance to put a face to the name while I gained some credibility. I was trained by one of the managers who worked on the project before hiring me. Once he saw that I was catching on quickly and making process improvements to the items he already implemented, he slowly pulled away from the project. He knew I was competent and no longer needed his direct support. If I did, I was not afraid to ask.

As I ran the project on my own, I was initially responsible for weekly check-ins. Gradually, that decreased to monthly check-ins and then to check-ins on an as-needed basis. Don't get me wrong: It was a steep learning curve because I had no industry knowledge for the rest of my work scope. I overcame that obstacle by submerging myself in computer-based training, asking my peers for guidance (the ones who were subject matter experts), asking my new supervisor to approve me taking external training courses, and more. Some of those on my team were helpful, while others tried to dictate my duties or make me feel as if I were incompetent when I asked for help.

In hindsight, I acknowledge I started to feel a bit discouraged at times. I shook off those feelings and put the pedal to the metal. I refused to allow my negative self-talk and self-doubt to prevent me from succeeding. Nor was I going to let my peers get inside of my head and cause me to feel unqualified because I did not bring the same level of knowledge to the table. Although I had no experience in that particular field at the time, I had other relevant experiences and skill sets that allowed me to thrive in unfamiliar territories.

So, I pushed and remained vigilant. I continued asking for external training, and while my supervisor allowed me to take a few, I was **ALWAYS** limited in the amount of training I could take in comparison to my Vanilla colleagues. I attribute that to the fact that I was the newest member on the team and did not have a background in regulations or years of industry experience in that specialized area. I was a small fish in a big pond. I did not let that stop me, though! I dug in my heels, learned my role to a 'T,' created my own damn job description for the position, and made sure the assignment was handled according to my specifications.

Even though they still had me categorized as an admin, I was doing the work of a professional. I was proving the company wrong because just like they hired me as an admin, it did not mean I was incapable of taking on more responsibilities and challenges. If I weren't competent, they wouldn't have moved me into higher positions, correct? The company was just being cheap, though. They had me doing the work of a professional without the pay to complement it. Then, every time I inquired about a salary increase to my supervisor, it was like a merry-go-round. Her excuses typically included things like, *"I'll get back to you," "I'm not sure," "I need to follow up with H.R.,"* and the list goes on and on. I just tallied up each excuse with the rest of the red flags I had on file in the back of my mind.

Chapter 10

Mindset Change

As 2019 came to a close, I found myself taking stock of how far I had come. It was a little over six years, with no significant change. All that time, I received a bunch of lip service without actions to back it up. I was made false promises by the company, but nothing materialized. It began to take a toll on my headspace and how much I wanted to continue putting in. Of course, I did my job because I was still getting paid, but I was reluctant to go above and beyond as I had done in the past. After all, they never really appreciate it, so what's the point?

It was time for a shift of mindset...

Walking into the office Monday through Friday became a drag. I dreaded being there, but I thank God for employment because it could have been worse. What used to be joy and fireworks became mundane and left me feeling as if I were having wisdom teeth pulled daily.

As I looked around, I saw myself as a mere splatter on a Vanilla society. The color of my skin, the texture of my hair, and everything else about me stood out. The Fortune 500 company talked a good game about "Inclusion and Diversity," but I often asked myself, *"Where are they?!"* All around me, I see Vanilla and Crème, with just a few Chocolate Drops scattered here and there. No one who looked like me or who I could identify with held high-ranking positions. The other Chocolate Drops worked twice as hard but remained stagnant in their careers. Why was that? Was it because we are Chocolate or that they deem us not worthy enough to climb the corporate ladder? If that were true, why did they feel confident in giving us the work but not the salary increases or outward recognition? Day by day, week by week, and year by year, we come to work and put a smile on our faces, just so the irritation doesn't show outwardly.

We interview for various positions and nail it during the interview, but when the results come back after deliberation, we find out we were not selected. *"At this time, we have chosen to go with another candidate who is more qualified,"* is the standard response. Does 'more qualified' mean better-suited, a superb ass-kisser, spouse, friend, alumni buddy, or drop-dead gorgeous?

For internal moves, we hear, *"Something fell through."* They don't dare let us know if we are even being considered for other roles. However, when we see the individual who got the position or promotion, they are not a minority. Instead, they are a brown-noser who barely does any work—and the vast majority knows that!

I ask myself: *"Where's the justice? What about fairness? Should I continue giving my best daily, compromising my morals and values at the expense of those who don't appreciate me?"* Although I genuinely care about my work, ethics, and the company, after being sidestepped, discredited, lied to, and belittled far too often, I fight against not developing a laid-back attitude—the type that says, ***"I don't give a flying bee about this company! I've done the bare minimum. That's enough. Just give me my paycheck on the 15th and 30th!"***

What about when your supervisor or manager says they've noticed a change? Hmm...I wonder why. If you are consistently giving your all and don't see any reward—a bonus, raise, or salary increase, for example—why should you continue busting your butt to make that person and the company look good? The whole point of people working is to create a nice lifestyle, have enough resources to live comfortably, and to take care of their obligations and responsibilities.

Believe me; I know how it can be at times. You put your all into something but encounter a lack of training and support, are expected to make miracles happen, and meet hard deadlines without recognition in pay or otherwise. Sometimes, you put up with it to ensure you have the resources needed to provide for your family. Eventually, the time comes when enough is enough, and you must pull the plug for your mental, emotional, and physical wellbeing.

What can be done to create relevant change? How can we change the way employers see certain things? How can we call out the B.S. *without* placing blame, all while spreading awareness on real issues? The change I am referring to is one that will be passed down for generations to come—the change that is legacy building...the change that no only changes actions but also thoughts...the change that is not based on unconscious biases and perceptions. I'm talking about an external change!

Perhaps a clean house is good. Get rid of all the people with old, orthodox, and stinking thinking in management or, at a minimum, hold them accountable by retraining them, aggressively evaluating them, and conditioning them with pay stipulations. Another option is to create an initiation by having various people who have faced numerous issues come forward for an engaging discussion. There is power in numbers!

If we don't address the underlying problems and bring them to the forefront, the cycle will always continue. We can't just talk about it in private with 'trusted' resources and then expect one person to be the spokesperson to fight all battles. It doesn't work like that. Upper management needs facts and numbers. They need to be hit where it hurts.

Stand up, my friends! We need a home run!

Oh, but wait... There's a flipside. The employees who come forward want to ensure they are not jeopardizing their jobs. They do not want to be retaliated against or have their performance review suffer. They need assurance that their efforts are not just another buy-in that will never truly get resolved. Some individuals have chosen to remain quiet and endure, while others leave without disclosing the real reasons for their departure. That is where H.R. and people of influence in the corporation should open their eyes and do some real investigations.

In the company I work for, they have begun hiring more experienced hires than ever before, but a lot of them are working for a short time and then leaving. Other employees are also leaving and going to competitors for a higher salary, workplace flexibility, advancement in their careers, etc. What does that tell you? As society is evolving, so is the workforce. Baby Boomers are retiring, and Generation X is in the phase where they are getting close to the end of their careers but are still willing to help train personnel when asked. Millennials are not buying the rigid conservatives, toxic work environments, and close-mindedness by those in authority, which gives them more time to spend with their families, better pay, the option to pursue graduate or doctorate degrees, entrepreneurship, and more.

So, if the workforce cannot appeal to all demographics, then we surely are in a crisis! We must savor the talent we have now, make credible changes, adapt to industry and societal changes, and gain new perspectives. Here's the thing: It needs to be done collectively with a strong team of leaders who aren't just going to talk about it, but also put their money where their mouth is.

At the time of this writing, the company I work for is starting to investigate new areas, such as external surveys like the Denison Organizational Culture Survey. Moreover, they don't even send out the survey to all personnel to avoid the data being skewed. They are bringing in subject matter experts to teach and review vast topics, but if everyone can't attend the seminars, then it's still an issue. It's a little too late for that because lots of talented people have already left the company, morale is low in various groups, and with the current political climate, things have intensified.

I'm sure you can see how the culture has shifted from 2013 to now. As for me, I see a culture change from the time I joined the company, and, in my opinion, it's not good.

Whew! Due to all the commotion, I took a vacation that was a little over three weeks. It's incredible how, when I took that extended break, I was welcomed back with, *"We thought you weren't coming back."* I chuckled and said, *"Well, if I had won the lottery, **I wouldn't have!**"*

I thought things would have died down or shifted with the onset of a new year/new decade while I was gone. Nope. I was wrong.

I settled back into work mode and tackled emails with questions that others were capable of answering on my behalf, but they didn't. While on vacation or out of the office, things could definitely pile up, especially if you aren't proactive and think ahead. Thankfully, I stayed one step ahead and made sure all the critical items were tended to before I left.

I rolled my eyes...back to reality. Same ole, same ole!

The questions and concerns I had before my vacation were left unanswered, leaving me to follow up consistently. The message that it sends to employees is that management doesn't care and that it is not a priority on their list, which only causes the staff to disengage and feel invaluable. Yes, we understand that everyone is busy with deliverables, etc., but when you have a little over three weeks to research personnel's concerns, and nothing gets done, there is an issue.

Salary, personnel development, and career roadmaps should be considered, especially if work keeps getting piled on without compensation or a change in classification level to be equivalent to the load. Money is not everything, but when financial burdens are weighing you down, and you have family obligations to fulfill, then anxiety and stress increase. Then, when your supervisor tells you that you aren't competent to do the work of a professional (but it's what you have been doing all along), it's like a slap in the face — a way for the company to brush you off and not give you what you are worth and deserve. They know what they're doing is wrong, but if you don't have a pitbull-like tenacity to fight for what's yours, then don't expect them to bring up the topic. They don't mind working you like a pack mule while they give you a little food and water to fuel your energy to keep you working a little harder.

You must speak up because, without a voice, no change will take place. Stop sweeping things under the rug and thinking, *"It will be revealed soon enough,"* because eight times out of ten, if you are silent, what do you think the next woman or man will do? Be the one to break the cycle. As it is said, ***"Closed mouths don't get fed!"***

Often, we are our own biggest critics. Our inner thoughts can cause us not to fight for ourselves or what is right because we are so busy worrying about what others will think or say about us. We must overcome fear, overlook unconscious biases, and be unafraid to speak up in a room where we are the only bold ones. Whether we choose to believe it or not, someone is counting on us to release our inner warrior. We can be the David who slays Goliath once and for all. We work just as hard as everyone else (sometimes, even moreso) because we constantly have to prove ourselves. Yes, our work should speak for itself, but we are judged on our mannerisms, body language, appearance, and other trivial factors that should not even matter...yet, they do.

Since it's done that way, let's make it a grand motion picture and give them something that will land us a Grammy Award!

Chapter 11

Curtains Finally Closing

It is said that patience is a virtue, but don't waste your time waiting on something that may never happen. Begin to evaluate your current situation and work on putting plans into play. Life does not stand still and wait for us to get it right. The clock is always ticking, and time is still moving.

In this long season of waiting for this company to do what's right or treat me fairly, I have missed out on fulfilling things that were important to me. I thought it was a waste at first, but my perspective has since changed. I have realized and now understand it was a season of cultivating me for my next destination. God wanted me to endure what I went through so that I could later write about it and bless the person reading my story now.

We are all equipped for various seasons in life, and, at the end of that season, there will be a set time for us to bloom and enjoy the fruits of our labor. Nothing is ever in vain. When it's all said and done, you will realize why you had to endure the trials and challenges. **Remember: God makes NO mistakes!**

Chapter 12

Self-Care:
Realizing You Matter, Too

Stop making everyone else and everything around you a priority. Make time for **YOU** and what really matters to **YOU**. How long are you going to forfeit what makes you happy? Are you just going through the motions of life, trying to get by, only to end up feeling burned out? If so, that is your body, mind, and soul speaking to you. Take a pause and actually listen.

That's what I did. I felt like I was on an emotional rollercoaster, fighting so hard to get what I deserved and what I worked so hard to obtain. I was full of anger and disappointment, to the point that I no longer cared. They kept putting more on me because they knew I was capable, but I received nothing in return.

Talk about modern-day slavery... No, we're not in the fields picking cotton and corn, but we are confined behind cubicle walls, taking commands from the 'Master.' They condition us to feel that we need just to sit there and take the abuse if we want our performance ranking to correlate, especially if we are in the admin bucket at a company that enforces ranking.

At first, I was all about work, my performance, and ranking. Then, I had a mental realization or spirit of discernment that showed me I was clearly being used mentally, physically, and emotionally. The job didn't care about me. If something were to happen to me (God forbid), they would quickly put up a job opening post.

If they did care, they would have taken into account I was no longer doing admin work and honored my degree (even if I did get it while working for them). They did, however, pay to assist with tuition reimbursement, but they didn't bump up my classification level or paygrade to complement my duties, performance, etc. The opportunity to take more external industry courses like my peers would have given me a competitive advantage, but I was denied. When I brought it to management's attention, they had all sorts of excuses. I will likely never know the difference between me (as a person with over six years of tenure, previous work experience, and a degree) in comparison with a new college graduate with no work experience. I know it's not right to compare myself to others, but you can't deny the validity of my point.

Today, I am working on loving me, spending more time with my family and friends, working only eight hours a day, and channeling my energy to other things that build me up. Self-care is essential. You must take time for yourself because if you don't, they won't think twice about burning you out. Your health will suffer due to stress, and then, you just end up not caring. I realized I didn't want to sink into depression or slip into a black hole. I did not want to continue carrying around the hurt, pain, anger, and be weighed down with grudges. It's not who God designed me to be.

Do not give up on your dreams. Someone is waiting for you to pass the baton to them. You were created for a purpose and, if you do not fulfill it, then someone else will suffer due to your lack of obedience. Every pain and struggle you endure will produce fruit. It will not be in vain. Get up and push past your fears and self-doubt. You can do anything you put your mind to. Don't let your naysayers or critics have the upper hand. People will always try to talk you out of something they were afraid of doing or didn't think they could achieve themselves. Nevertheless, your race is for you and no one else.

Run like you have no care in the world and reach for those things that may be unreachable for others but within your limits.

When we start comparing ourselves to others, we begin to lose our identity. We were all created for a purpose and have our own destiny assignments. Take some time and find out what you were placed on this earth to do. When you do, everything in and around you will form a beautiful synergy. Things will start to line up in your favor, you will be able to see things clearer, hear God more, and the utmost peace you feel will be inexplainable.

Just because someone appears to be successful and happy on the surface doesn't always mean that everything else around them is peachy. They could be catching hell at home while smiling in your face. So, don't put them on a pedestal and think that if you achieve what they have, then you will be happy. What is for you will be for you, and **no one** can take that away.

Run your own race and be content with yourself. I pray you find your divine purpose and assignment while here on this earth and work on being the best "you" possible. Study the Word of God and listen to those inner thoughts that are fruitful and peaceful. Slowly but surely, the pieces of the puzzle will begin to fit. It takes time, but it's well worth the effort. Without hope, you are subjected to fear and hopelessness. Once you have been beaten down so much, they expect you to just give up instead of fight for justice. The number of hoops you must jump through when you are a minority amongst a race that feels superior is quite distasteful. As a society, we can't move forward if we keep replaying history.

What are evident changes you can make today that will hold true and create a cosmic effect for future generations to come? Why sit when you can stand? Why remain silent when you were blessed with a mouth to speak? Why not write when you were given hands to create? Stop shrinking back and start blasting off! You were created for greatness!

It takes courage to stand and fight for justice. It takes courage to challenge authority when you know they are screwing you over. It takes courage to call out unconscious biases. It takes courage to have those difficult conversations with management and hold them accountable. It takes courage to step out on **FAITH**. It takes courage to walk into your destiny and purpose calling. It takes courage to speak up when everyone else is telling you to be quiet. It takes courage to be **YOU**...your *AUTHENTIC* self.

Chapter 13

2020: Far from Perfect Vision, But A Slap of Reality

2020 was supposed to be the year of perfect vision, clarity, and big things happening. However, God had other plans and threw us all a curveball. The year was far from anything perfect. Many people faced ups and downs, including dealing with a global pandemic, high death rates, job loss, long-time businesses permanently shutting their doors, and more. It was a challenging year, but some people rolled with the punches and learned how to pivot. They took the cards they were dealt and created for themselves new opportunities. It is just like the adage states, *"When life gives you lemons, you got to make lemonade!"*

As for me, most notably, I have learned nothing in life is guaranteed and that when it comes down to staying afloat, some people can be outright grimy and gruesome. They will do whatever they need to "save face," making virtually any given situation a battlefield and dog-eat-dog territory. My only advice is not to sacrifice your morals and values for the appeasement of another's validation. All it will do is cause you pain and guilt in the long run because deep down, we all know what is right.

The good, the bad, and the ugly. I have definitely experienced my fair share of them all. However, I do believe everything happens for a reason and that it is up to us to control our reactions to each situation we face. We can either become a part of the solution or fuel the fire and create a bigger problem.

After hearing *"NO"* for so long when it came to my needs and desires for wanting to be converted from an OCA to an MPT, it finally happened after I took a **BOLD** and **COURAGEOUS** step during the early stages of the Black Lives Matter (BLM) Movement check-in with the V.P. He asked those of us who identified as being "Black"/"African American" to speak on our experiences—which was a shocking number because there weren't many of us. In fact, there were less than 30 Chocolate Drops available to share our stories of being faced with racism in both personal and professional settings. Some people volunteered to share openly, while others were called on (I was one of the latter). By that point, I was already mentally checked-out and said to myself, *"Enough is **ENOUGH**!"* When my time came, I did not hold back.

The shock to my system was the representation (or lack thereof) of us Chocolate Drops. It seemed as though there were just enough of us in the department for them to check a box showing they were, indeed, inclusive and diverse. Out of that population, there were only two managers and two supervisors. That's not an alarming statistic, but I had to wonder if they were there just to be "token" holders. The company has a ways to go with inclusion and diversity. If they are willing to put in the work, then I can see some things changing. It will be a long ride, though.

Moving along…

One week after sharing my experiences with racism, my supervisor called me to say they were converting me to MPT. I was no longer in the little leagues! On June 24, 2020, I went from a CL15 to a CL22, along with a 20% salary increase! *(That goes to show I was underpaid by 20% in comparison to my peers.)* I was hoping they would have given me back pay for the years I was underpaid, but that is too much like the **right** thing to do. Nonetheless, I was grateful for the increase — **but why did it take so long?** I had been with the company for seven years, with four of them possessing my B.S. degree, and it was my second professional role (per se).

Thoughts and questions began to flood my mind. Was I given the increase in pay as hush money, meaning they were trying to clean up their act as it related to correcting pay disparities with their minorities? After all, big corporations were starting to be faced with questions regarding what they were doing on the inclusion and diversity fronts. They were being asked how they were responding to BLM, if they were giving Blacks positions, and what career development looked like for minorities. So, did they **genuinely** feel I deserved the increase and, if so, why didn't they back pay me for the years I was incorrectly compensated due to improper categorization? I had the work experience plus a Bachelor's degree, which was in stark contrast to some of my peers with no degree. Was their action in response to me speaking up in a group setting where everyone heard how they were treating me, and they felt bad? Was the increase given just to save face and prevent me from opening a case against the company, especially since the BLM was a hot topic and claims and other courses of action were being brought up?

I ask you to take a moment to consider the validity of my questions. Are they warranted? The reverse could have also been true: The title change and subsequent salary increase were done out of the goodness of management's heart.

When the H.R. representative did a follow-up with me, I expressed my feelings concerning the situation as a whole. Yes, I was grateful for the increase but felt it was not given genuinely and based on my merits. She reassured me that it was being reworked behind the scenes for some time before the change *(correction!)* being made to my position.

Oh! I cannot fail to mention how, after my supervisor delivered the "good news," she revealed that more would be expected of me due to the promotion. In my opinion, I was not granted a **promotion**. My job title and duties remained the same, with the only change being my salary increase (something that needed to be done in light of being underpaid in comparison to my peers). I was the only one on my team classified as an OCA, as well as the only "Chocolate Drop/Black/African American." I also had visual proof that was shown in a meeting with the different classification levels of the group that started at CL22. My CL-level was nowhere close to that. In addition, a Tier-2 manager told me he was shocked that I was a CL15.

So, if you read between the lines, what does **that** tell you?

Hmm… It's just a reminder to be wise as a serpent but harmless as a dove and to always do your due diligence.

During that time, not only was I dealing with social injustice, fighting systemic racism, doing my best to stay safe during the global pandemic, etc., but my dad was also sick. He fell ill in May, which was difficult for me. I had to make a lifestyle change and began to work remotely. My family needed me, and I needed to ensure I would not put anyone at risk by going into the office where it was an open workspace (some ignorant people were taking COVID-19 as a joke, refusing to follow safety protocols.) As I am sure you can imagine, I had a lot on my mind and my plate, but I managed because I knew things still needed to get done.

While I was working remotely, the company started to change things and even questioned my work process. At first, it was annoying. I didn't think much of it and just rolled with the punches. Since the inception of my new role, my work processes were being challenged by the need to automate, revamp my working relationships, etc. It must be noted here that the position was brand-new, so there was no background information. I had to make the role what it is today, based on what I have learned along the way. It wasn't always easy, but I needed to do what I had to do.

Change is good, but when you know how things work and understand your client, I believe if things are working great, why step in the ant pile and stir up a mess?

To keep the peace, I went along with the changes to appease them and to show I was a team player so that they wouldn't use it against me, especially since it was already mentioned that I was in the "big leagues" now. I was informed that things were going to be more competitive and that I had to see the big picture — instead of just being task-oriented, trying to get things done without questioning if there could be a better way, or suggest the implementation of new strategies for sustainability.

What used to take me a short amount of time soon began to take a lot longer due to the change in processes. Also, I had to deal with service providers who were no longer working in their offices due to COVID. It was essential to have understanding and compassion because everyone was dealing with something, whether personal or professional, and it took a toll mentally, physically, and emotionally.

For months, I endured the changes that life brought my way. Then, the holidays came, along with the urgency to close out quarterly "stuff," the pressure of being unable to travel or do the things I wanted due to COVID restrictions, etc. As a nation, people found themselves completely isolated, and they were on edge and irritable. Totally not a good mix.

So, the holidays were extremely difficult for me. After taking care of my dad for months and spending quality time with him, he passed away on November 25th — the day before Thanksgiving. Then, almost a week later, I found out on December 1st that I would be laid off effective mid-February 2021. When I heard the news, I was a little shocked and in disbelief. My supervisor was surprised by how well I took the news, but I kind of suspected something like that was coming my way, which made the moment bittersweet. Still, hearing bad news two weeks in a row sucked. However, life is about 80% of how you react and only 20% of the situation.

Overall, my job decided to cut approximately 1,900 jobs. Before getting the news, three people on my team (including me) were in the involuntary lay-off bucket.

I was the **only** one to be let go and, coincidentally, the only Black person (the other two ended up getting new job titles/advanced roles on the team).

At first, I was a little bitter about the whole thing—until I remembered that **GOD** has the final say. **HE** is the one in control. I began to thank Him and proclaim, *"When one door closes, another one always opens. Everything happens for a reason."* Just like seasons change, so must we. I know better things are on the horizon for me, and to be honest, I was looking for a way out prior to the news. Will I begin another job with more pay? Will I start my own business? Time will tell. For now, I appreciate the opportunity to pivot again and address my three Rs:

Refuel

Refocus

Realign

I will also take some time to **R**elax, **R**elate, and **R**elease because **this** Queen is coming back better than before!

So, to recap: I was called on to speak about my experiences and feelings relating to the Black Lives Matter Movement, George Floyd murder, etc. A week after sharing my transparent viewpoint, I received a 20% pay increase. Although grateful for the increase, justice would have included receiving back pay for the three years prior where I was underpaid compared to my White colleagues—not to mention it was my second professional role with the company.

In life, we all endure various trials and tribulations, but how we react to them can determine how we can create a healthy perspective and enable good things to occur. We go through a variety of seasons in life, with each giving us a particular lesson to learn. It helps to understand that things aren't permanent and, if we deal with the temporary, it will set us up for success.

Change your mindset and perspective to channel positivity and create opportunities out of the negatives. Then, when you leave a job, do so on a good note with your head held high and dignity intact. Leave them wishing they wouldn't have made the decision they did. Although you may be gone, the impact and lives you touch along the way will leave a residue and remnants of you for them to ponder for years to come.

So, cheers to ending chapters and beginning new ones! Be your authentic self — the one who knocks down barriers, rises above limitations, and takes leaps of faith that help you walk out your purpose!

Conclusion

As I went about my daily life of being a Chocolate Drop in Corporate America, the things that used to matter started to fade away and lose their relevance. After all, being a minority in the vast world of Vanilla Drops is always and will always be a competition. We need to come together as a society and stop letting the color of our skin tear us apart. At the end of the day, we all have red blood running through our veins, so I don't know why we are so divided. We are divided by race, gender, creed, religion, administrative assistants, technicians, engineers, chemists, geologists, geophysics, and so forth. Conversely, we are all educated, talented, intelligent, wise, and capable of learning new things. Why, then, can't the playing field be equal?

Each of us has something valuable to bring to the table. In fact, when we all leverage each other's knowledge and expertise, it can create a unison that gives us a competitive advantage. We are better when we are united, which is why change can start with you and me! We can work to promote culture change, call out unconscious bias, take a stand together, tell our stories versus remaining quiet and scared, and give others a fighting chance. If we change our perspectives and encourage others to do the same, it will create a domino effect where others can follow suit.

In the workforce, it's up to the head honcho and their subordinates to positively reinforce a new culture and be receptive to seeing how things work differently. It's imperative that we hold them accountable. Besides, we are stakeholders in the corporation, too. If we begin to leave en masse and go mainstream, people will take notice and start asking questions that get to the root of the problem. Surely, they don't want their brand tainted, so it will force them to tighten up. With no real or evident change, the vicious cycle will continue.

At the time of this writing, the year is 2020. We would think things have improved, but some people still have color, segregation, cast systems, and so forth so ingrained in them, they can't shake it. To them, they think it's good, but their ways only prove to diminish companies' presence in any given industry. Progression is a struggle because when things are deeply rooted in someone's core, they must first want to change. Hiding behind a mask can only suffice for so long before their actions reflect their true nature. An unfortunate result of their actions is that their antics and bad behaviors taint the rest of the workforce, especially since some people tend to mimic what others do—whether right or wrong.

You can't change the way people treat you, but you can shift the way people perceive you. As well, you don't have to continue tolerating how others behave towards you. Thank God, the United States is a country that allows us to have the freedom to make choices. We can leave a job, find another job, create a job, and tap into other ways to leverage multiple streams of income. You have options! You possess the willpower to create and determine if you will remain in a situation that only drains your energy and sucks the life out of you. Therefore, when you go to work daily, the last thing you should desire is being miserable.

To overcome those feelings, you must *Refuel*, *Realign*, and *Refocus*. You can do so by using your story and testimony to help set someone else free. Don't be afraid to share what you've been through. You did not endure those trials and tribulations just to shrink back and remain quiet. Someone needs to hear your story to strengthen them and help them navigate through the trenches to avoid engaging in the same things you have.

That is why I started to live Boldly and Beautifully. I realized I matter and that I bring something useful to the table. Self-care became my priority as I walked into my divine assignment and purpose while here on earth. I take pleasure in helping others and now have immeasurable peace. Out of my frustrations, they encouraged me to give birth to this book to help educate others to see things from my untainted lens. You may be able to relate to much of what was penned here. It is my hope that you have been inspired to educate others to change their frame of mind.

I leave you with the following:

Don't spend too much time building up someone else's dreams and visions that you neglect your own. You matter, too. Your time is just as valuable as someone else's. Listen to that still, small voice. Don't let your gifts and talents go to waste. Tap into your inner calling because you can achieve your wildest dreams with the right game plan.

Be blessed and prosperous! Until we meet and see each other next time, do **YOU** because nobody else can replicate **YOU**. You *ARE* uniquely made!

Reflection Quotes

❖ Some people don't want you to succeed and will do whatever they can to keep you down. When you recognize that person (or company) does not have your best interest at heart, start making moves to find something that is a better fit.

❖ Don't waste your valuable time trying to fit in where you were never meant to be long term. Seasons and times change, so recognize when your time is up and when you are being called to higher things.

❖ Share your experiences. When we talk about our trials and tribulations, it helps others. Let's learn from other people's mistakes, be open to new perspectives, and support one another. No one **WINS** alone. It takes a community, courage, and a buy-in to create change.

❖ We are **ALL** leaders. Each of us has a respective audience to reach.

❖ Sometimes, people place limitations on you because they do not want you to outshine them, or there is a sense of jealousy or another complex issue. Let's help build up one another instead of tearing each other down.

❖ People may see you one way, but they don't know all the struggles, trials, and tribulations you had to go through to get where you are.

❖ Don't judge a book by its cover. Go beyond the surface and gain wisdom. We are all guilty of passing judgment on others. (That is something I, for one, need to work on and hope others will, too.)

❖ Stop wasting your valuable time with people who will never appreciate what you bring to the table or have to offer.

❖ Stop waiting for your company to change the way they treat you. Instead, start looking for other opportunities or ways to capitalize on your God-given talents and skills.

❖ Stop waiting for someone to cosign your dreams. Start running with passion. In time, the right people who genuinely care and want to support you will fall into place.

❖ Let's continue to encourage one another to be the best version of ourselves that we possibly can. Take a break from all the hustle and bustle, get in tune with your inner self, meditate, and release stress by working out, listening to music, or unplugging from the everyday madness in this world.

❖ Some people just need someone to believe in them and give them a chance, and they will put in the work.

❖ Hearing "NO" is just a redirection to your real purpose in life. It is meant to push you to evaluate your skills and start thinking about what you could start working on to advance in life.

❖ If you have a dream and vision to achieve something, then you have the POWER to do it! Keep the determination and continue to run your race. You may fall or even fail, but that that doesn't mean you can't achieve greatness. Get back up and press forward.

Discovery Exercise: Who Am I?

W ho am I? I am a professional who now knows her life's purpose. It is not to sit down, muzzle my mouth, and continually let people get over on me. I know my worth. It's time to speak up, activate my faith, and walk into the destiny God has for my life.

~~~~~~~~~~

I encourage you to take a leap of faith and get out of your comfort zone. If you are wondering what you should do next, take a step back and write down all the things you are good at doing. Out of those things, which ones bring you joy and fulfillment? How can you make a change in not just your life but also the lives of those in your community and beyond? Formulate a plan on how you can implement those things and still bring revenue into your household. Times are changing, and one thing's for sure; jobs can come and go, but the empire and legacy you build will **ALWAYS** be in existence, as long as you have a strong foundation and continue to cultivate it. You, too, can be all the things you ever imagined, so stop limiting yourself by the things people say you cannot do or by operating under the limitations that others have placed on you.

About the Author

Genesis Amaris Kemp is a wife, sister, aunt, cousin, friend, and child of God. She is bubbly, loves to talk, loves to try new things, travel, meet new people, and encourage others the best she can.

Genesis is the youngest of four siblings with a vast cultural background. She began writing in high school off and on as her way to release stress and express herself. It was also her way of communicating with God. In a sense, she felt as if she was unable to talk to those closest to her. She knew if she told her problems to the family, they would see it as nagging or constantly complaining. Instead of internalizing her issues and unsettling battles that could lead to depression and oppression, the Holy Spirit led her to write. Getting her thoughts out of her head and onto paper proved therapeutic. Little did she know that would lead to her writing a book.

Some might say she has no qualifications to write a book, but when you go through experiences in life, you don't need particular skills to deem you worthy. Life experiences alone can paint some vivid pictures because we all go through various trials and tribulations that resonate with others. As such, each area of Genesis' life was a lesson that shaped her into the woman she is today. She allowed God to take her gifts and talents and make them extraordinary. She is continually learning what her destiny and purpose assignments are while on this earth, all while embracing her writing passion.

Genesis is a woman of color who said, "Enough is enough," and is now bolder than ever. She tried to remain quiet, but that didn't work because no change occurred. Today, she is readapting to the current times and making some life-changing decisions. She is stepping outside of her comfort zone by speaking up, challenging the status quo, and refusing to let limitations placed on her keep her down.

Genesis sees herself as a visionary and a woman who will go on to do great things that empower others to speak up for themselves. Yes, it may be hard; yes, it may hurt. In the long run, she desires to encourage others to help those who may not have a voice. She is a trailblazer who wants others to live out their dreams, goals, and visions. If it takes her writing this book to accomplish those tasks, then so be it. We all have been given a wonderful purpose in life. It is up to us to walk it out and live victoriously!

Genesis Amaris Kemp